Math Mammoth
Grade 1 Review Workbook

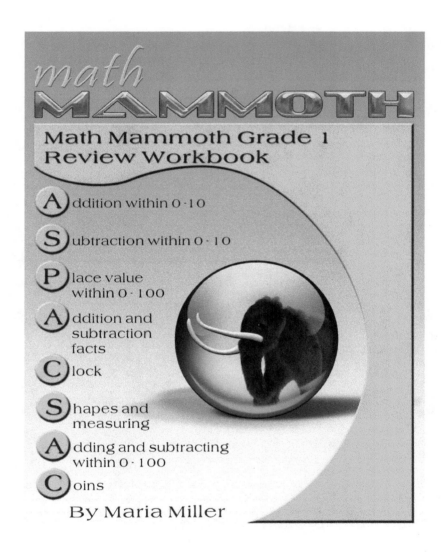

By Maria Miller

Copyright 2018 Maria Miller
ISBN 978-1-942715-42-9

Edition 6/2018

Math Mammoth Grade 1 Review Workbook
Contents

Introduction

Math Mammoth Grade 1 Review Workbook is intended to give students a thorough review of first grade math, following the main areas of Common Core Standards for grade 1 mathematics. The book has both topical as well as mixed (spiral) review worksheets, and includes both topical tests and a comprehensive end-of-the-year test. The tests can also be used as review worksheets, instead of tests.

You can use this workbook for various purposes: for summer math practice, to keep a child from forgetting math skills during other break times, to prepare students who are going into second grade, or to give first grade students extra practice during the school year.

The topics reviewed in this workbook are:

- addition within 0 - 10
- subtraction within 0 - 10
- place value within 0 - 100
- addition and subtraction facts
- clock
- shapes and measuring
- adding and subtracting within 0 - 100
- coins

In addition to the topical reviews and tests, the workbook also contains some cumulative (spiral) review pages.

The content for these is taken from *Math Mammoth Grade 1 Complete Curriculum*, so naturally this workbook works especially well to prepare students for grade 2 in Math Mammoth. However, the content follows a typical study for grade 1, so this workbook can be used no matter which math curriculum you follow.

Please note this book does not contain lessons or instruction for the topics. It is not intended for initial teaching. It also will not work if the student needs to completely re-study these topics (the student has not learned the topics at all). For that purpose, please consider *Math Mammoth Grade 1 Complete Curriculum*, which has all the necessary instruction and lessons.

I wish you success with teaching math!

Maria Miller, the author

Addition Within 0-10 Review

1. Write different sums of 5 and sums of 6.

$5 =$ _____ $+$ _____ $6 =$ _____ $+$ _____

$5 =$ _____ $+$ _____ $6 =$ _____ $+$ _____

$5 =$ _____ $+$ _____ $6 =$ _____ $+$ _____

$5 =$ _____ $+$ _____ $6 =$ _____ $+$ _____

2. Draw a line to the correct answer.

$4 + 1$
$2 + 3$
$3 + 3$
$5 + 0$
5        $4 + 2$ 6
$5 + 1$
$0 + 6$
$1 + 4$
$2 + 4$

3. Find the missing addends

_____ $+ 2 = 6$ _____ $+ 0 = 6$

$2 +$ _____ $= 5$ $0 +$ _____ $= 5$

$1 +$ _____ $= 5$ $3 +$ _____ $= 6$

$6 +$ _____ $= 6$ $4 +$ _____ $= 6$

_____ $+ 1 = 6$ _____ $+ 4 = 5$

4. Compare. Write $<$, $>$ or $=$.

$2 + 2$ ☐ 5 $4 + 4$ ☐ 5 6 ☐ $2 + 4$

$2 + 3$ ☐ 5 $5 + 5$ ☐ 5 6 ☐ $2 + 5$

$2 + 4$ ☐ 5 $5 + 0$ ☐ 5 6 ☐ $2 + 6$

5. Write different sums of 7 and sums of 8.

7 = _____ + _____	8 = _____ + _____
7 = _____ + _____	8 = _____ + _____
7 = _____ + _____	8 = _____ + _____
7 = _____ + _____	8 = _____ + _____
7 = _____ + _____	8 = _____ + _____
7 = _____ + _____	8 = _____ + _____

6. Draw a line to the
   correct answer.

7   4 + 3
        2 + 6
        3 + 5
        4 + 4
        5 + 2   8
        1 + 6
        5 + 3
        7 + 1
        6 + 2

7. Find the missing addends

_____ + 2 = 7   _____ + 4 = 8

_____ + 4 = 7   3 + _____ = 7

2 + _____ = 8   3 + _____ = 8

5 + _____ = 8   7 + _____ = 8

6 + _____ = 7   5 + _____ = 7

8. Compare. Write < , > or = .

3 + 3 ☐ 7	6 + 1 ☐ 7	8 ☐ 6 + 4
4 + 3 ☐ 7	6 + 6 ☐ 7	8 ☐ 4 + 4
5 + 3 ☐ 7	6 + 4 ☐ 7	8 ☐ 5 + 4

9. Write different sums of 9 and sums of 10.

9 = _____ + _____	10 = _____ + _____
9 = _____ + _____	10 = _____ + _____
9 = _____ + _____	10 = _____ + _____
9 = _____ + _____	10 = _____ + _____
9 = _____ + _____	10 = _____ + _____
9 = _____ + _____	10 = _____ + _____

10. Draw a line to the correct answer.

$$2 + 7$$
$$3 + 6$$
$$4 + 6$$
$$5 + 5$$
9     $$9 + 1$$ 10
$$1 + 8$$
$$5 + 4$$
$$3 + 7$$
$$2 + 8$$

11. Find the missing addends

_____ $+ 2 = 10$ _____ $+ 6 = 9$

_____ $+ 4 = 9$ $7 +$ _____ $= 10$

$2 +$ _____ $= 9$ $3 +$ _____ $= 9$

$5 +$ _____ $= 10$ $7 +$ _____ $= 9$

$6 +$ _____ $= 10$ $4 +$ _____ $= 10$

12. Compare. Write < , > or = .

$2 + 6$ ☐ 9 $6 + 6$ ☐ 10 10 ☐ $10 + 4$

$4 + 6$ ☐ 9 $5 + 5$ ☐ 10 10 ☐ $10 + 0$

$3 + 6$ ☐ 9 $4 + 4$ ☐ 10 10 ☐ $10 + 7$

13. Add.

a.	b.	c.
8 + 1 = _____	4 + 1 + 1 = _____	5 + 2 + 0 + 0 = _____
6 + 2 = _____	8 + 2 + 0 = _____	4 + 3 + 1 + 2 = _____
1 + 7 = _____	1 + 3 + 6 = _____	1 + 2 + 2 + 1 = _____
3 + 4 = _____	2 + 2 + 4 = _____	2 + 3 + 1 + 3 = _____

14. Fill in the addition table as much as you can.

+	2	4	3	6	7	5	8
1							
3							
4							
2							

Puzzle Corner $\triangle$ represents a number, and $\square$ represents another number. Solve what they are in each case (a, b, and c).

Hint: Make a guess! Then check if your guess is correct. If not, change your guess.

a.	b.	c.
$\triangle + \triangle = 6$	$\square + \triangle = 7$	$\square + \triangle + \triangle = 7$
$\square + \triangle = 8$	$\square + \square = 10$	$\square + \triangle = 5$

8

Addition Within 0-10 Test

1. Add.

a.	b.	c.	d.	e.	f.
2 + 4	8 + 1	6 + 2	8 + 2	5 + 4	6 + 3

2. Compare. Write $<$, $>$, or $=$.

a. 5 ☐ 6	c. 6 + 1 ☐ 10	e. 3 ☐ 1 + 0	g. 8 ☐ 6 + 3
b. 2 ☐ 9	d. 2 + 3 ☐ 5	f. 10 ☐ 0 + 6	h. 7 ☐ 2 + 5

3. Draw more. Write an addition sentence.

a. _____ + _____ = 10

b. _____ + _____ = 7

c. _____ + _____ = 10

4. Find the missing numbers.

a. $2 + $ _____ $= 7$ b. $1 + $ _____ $= 4$ c. $4 + $ _____ $= 10$ d. _____ $+ 7 = 9$

5. Solve the word problems.

a. Anna has seven stuffed animals and Abby has three. How many do they have in total?	b. Andy has eight pairs of shorts. Two of them are in the wash. How many are not?

Subtraction Within 0-10 Review

1. Write a fact family to match the picture.

_____ + _____ = _____   _____ – _____ = _____

_____ + _____ = _____   _____ – _____ = _____

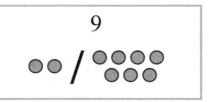

2. **a.** Write a subtraction that matches the addition 6 + 4 = 10.   _____ – _____ = _____

   b. Write a subtraction that matches the addition 5 + ____ = 9.   _____ – _____ = _____
   Also solve the addition.

3. **a.** There are 8 children playing in the yard. Two are girls.
   How many are boys?

   b. Kay has four marbles. Susan has two more marbles than Kay.
   Draw Kay's and Susan's marbles.

   c. Five sparrows and two robins are feeding on seeds. One more robin flies in.
   How many more sparrows than robins are there now?

4. Find the missing numbers.

a.	b.	c.	d.
3 + _____ = 4	6 – 3 = _____	10 – 0 = _____	8 – 2 = _____
1 + _____ = 9	8 – 5 = _____	5 – 3 = _____	7 – 3 = _____
3 + _____ = 10	7 – 6 = _____	6 – 6 = _____	10 – 1 = _____
2 + _____ = 7	10 – 8 = _____	7 – 4 = _____	9 – 2 = _____

Subtraction Within 0-10 Test

1. Write the fact family to match the picture.

_____ + _____ = _____   _____ + _____ = _____

_____ − _____ = _____   _____ − _____ = _____

8

2. **a.** Write a subtraction sentence that matches the addition $5 + 4 = 9$, using the same numbers.

_____ − _____ = _____

b. Solve the addition $6 +$ _____ $= 10$ and write a subtraction that matches the addition.

_____ − _____ = _____

3. **a.** There are 9 animals playing in the yard. Three are dogs and the rest are cats. How many cats are there?

b. Lisa has four more balls than Kelly.
Kelly has five balls.
Draw Kelly's and Lisa's balls.

c. Five robins and two sparrows are feeding on seeds.
Two more robins fly in. Now how many more robins are there than sparrows?

4. Find the missing numbers.

a. $4 +$ _____ $= 6$	**b.** $9 -$ _____ $= 3$	**c.** $9 - 0 =$ _____	**d.** $6 - 5 =$ _____
$1 +$ _____ $= 8$	$7 -$ _____ $= 5$	$7 - 1 =$ _____	$3 - 2 =$ _____
$5 +$ _____ $= 10$	_____ $- 1 = 6$	$9 - 7 =$ _____	$4 - 4 =$ _____
$6 +$ _____ $= 9$	_____ $- 2 = 4$	$8 - 2 =$ _____	$10 - 7 =$ _____

Mixed Review 1

1. Draw arrows to show the addition and the subtractions.

a. 6 + 2 = _____

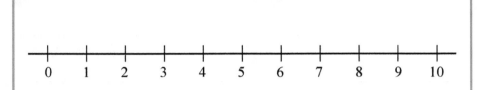

b. 9 − 4 = _____

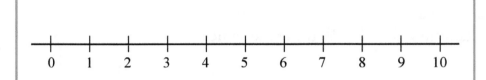

c. 7 − 3 = _____

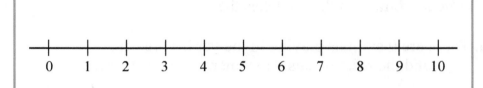

2. Make an addition sentence and a subtraction sentence from the same picture.

a. ●●●●○○○○○○

_____ + _____ = _____

_____ − _____ = _____

b. □□□□□▨▨▨

_____ + _____ = _____

_____ − _____ = _____

3. Add. Remember, you can add in any order.

a.
```
   2
   1
 + 4
```

b.
```
   5
   1
 + 4
```

c.
```
   2
   1
 + 1
```

d.
```
   6
   1
 + 2
```

e.
```
   4
   0
 + 3
```

4. Fill in the missing numbers.

a. 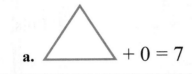 $+ 0 = 7$ b. $\triangle - 2 = 4$ c. $8 - \triangle = 1$

5. Compare. Write $<$, $>$, or $=$.

a. $2 + 3 \;\square\; 5$ c. $7 - 1 \;\square\; 9$ e. $2 \;\square\; 4 - 2$

b. $6 + 1 \;\square\; 8$ d. $4 - 4 \;\square\; 0$ f. $9 \;\square\; 9 - 1$

6. Find the missing numbers.

a.	b.	c.	d.
$6 + 4 =$ ____	$2 + 7 =$ ____	$3 +$ ____ $= 10$	$2 +$ ____ $= 9$
$4 + 4 =$ ____	$5 + 3 =$ ____	$3 +$ ____ $= 8$	$2 +$ ____ $= 7$

7. Draw the missing marbles to match the addition sentence.

a. $6 + 1 +$ ____ $= 10$

b. $1 + 4 +$ ____ $= 8$

8. Write the fact families.

a. Numbers: 9, 5, 4

____ $+$ ____ $=$ ____

____ $+$ ____ $=$ ____

____ $-$ ____ $=$ ____

____ $-$ ____ $=$ ____

b. Numbers: 10, 2, 8

____ $+$ ____ $=$ ____

____ $+$ ____ $=$ ____

____ $-$ ____ $=$ ____

____ $-$ ____ $=$ ____

9. Draw marbles for the child that has none.

[ ] Jane	[●●●●●●●●] Luis
[●●●●●●] Greg	[ ] Henry
a. Jane has 2 more than Greg.	**b.** Luis has 4 more than Henry.
[ ] Jill	[ ] Jim
[●●●●●●●] Bill	[●●●●] Ann
c. Jill has 2 fewer than Bill.	**d.** Ann has 3 fewer than Jim.

10. Solve.

a. Three children were playing. Then, five more children came to play.
Then, one child left. Now how many children are playing?

b. Judy has 3 marbles and Annie has 7.
How many marbles do the girls have together?

How many more does Annie have than Judy?

c. Kyle has 10 toy trucks. Some are blue and seven are black.
How many are blue?

d. Leah has 6 dollars. She wants to buy a book for $9.
How much more money does she need?

e. Matt has 10 socks and he can't find any of them! Then, he found three socks
under the bed and five in the closet. How many socks did Matt find?

How many are still missing?

Place Value Within 0-100 Review

1. Name the numbers using numbers and words.

    a. 1 ten 5 ones   _15_   _____

    b. 6 tens 7 ones   _____   _____

    c. 4 tens 0 ones   _____   _____

    d. 10 tens 0 ones   _____   _____

    e. 5 tens 1 one   _____   _____

2. Fill in the numbers on the number lines.

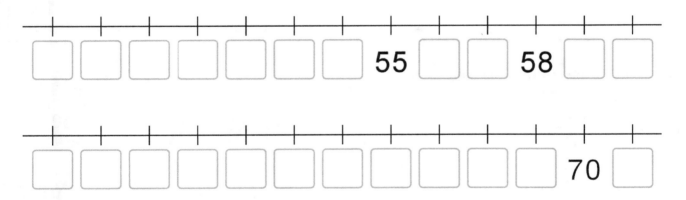

3. Circle the number that is *more*.

a.	**b.**	**c.**	**d.**	**e.**
78 87	22 25	56 57	68 80	101 11

4. Count. You can also do this orally with your teacher.

97, 98, _____, _____, _____, _____, _____,

_____, _____, _____, _____, _____, _____.

5. Break the numbers into their tens and ones.

a. 45 = 40 + 5	b. 25 = _____ + ____	c. 78 = _____ + ____
68 = _____ + ____	54 = _____ + ____	91 = _____ + ____

6. Build the numbers.

a. 50 + 7 = _____	b. 8 + 10 = _____	c. 90 + 6 = _____
20 + 0 = _____	9 + 70 = _____	9 + 60 = _____

7. Put the numbers in order.

a. 57, 17, 75	b. 18, 48, 44, 41
_____ < _____ < _____	_____ < _____ < _____ < _____

8. Compare the expressions and write < , > or = .

a. 56 ☐ 5 + 60

b. 20 + 8 ☐ 33

c. 60 + 5 ☐ 50 + 6

d. 34 ☐ 30 + 6

e. 4 + 90 ☐ 49

f. 80 + 2 ☐ 70 + 9

9. Skip-count. (You can also do this orally with your teacher.)

a. 13, 15, 17, _____, _____, _____, _____, _____, _____

b. _____, _____, _____, _____, _____, _____, 78, 88, 98

c. _____, _____, _____, _____, _____, 55, 60, 65, _____

Mystery Number

I have five less ones than 39, and one more ten than 47.

16

Place Value Within 0-100 Test

1. Name the numbers (with words).

   a. 1 ten 6 ones _____

   c. 7 tens 8 ones _____

   b. 5 tens 1 ones _____

   d. 9 tens 0 ones _____

2. Fill in the missing numbers on the number line.

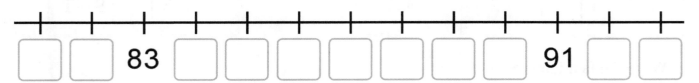

3. Break the numbers into tens and ones.

a. $45 = 40 + 5$	b. $52 = $ _____ $ + $ ____	c. $97 = $ _____ $ + $ ____
$86 = $ _____ $ + $ ____	$32 = $ _____ $ + $ ____	$19 = $ _____ $ + $ ____

4. Do the same the other way around! Add.

a.	**b.**	**c.**	**d.**
$20 + 9 = $ _____	$5 + 70 = $ _____	$2 + 80 = $ _____	$1 + 90 = $ _____

5. Put the numbers in order from smallest to greatest.

a. 75, 71, 57	**b.** 69, 98, 96	**c.** 81, 84, 49
____ $<$ ____ $<$ ____	____ $<$ ____ $<$ ____	____ $<$ ____ $<$ ____

6. Compare and write $<$, $>$, or $=$.

   a. 65 ☐ $5 + 60$ **b.** 43 ☐ $60 + 4$ **c.** $90 + 3$ ☐ $30 + 9$

Mixed Review 2

1. Break the numbers into tens and ones.

a. 22 = _____ + _____	**b.** 64 = _____ + _____	**c.** 95 = _____ + _____

2. Compare. Write $<$, $>$, or $=$.

a. $2 + 3$ ☐ $5 + 1$	**c.** $8 - 2$ ☐ 4	**e.** 6 ☐ $4 + 2$
b. $6 + 4$ ☐ $8 + 2$	**d.** $7 - 4$ ☐ 5	**f.** 8 ☐ $9 - 1$

3. Write the fact families.

a. $\quad 3 \; + \; 7 \; = \; \_\_\_\_$ $\_\_\_\_ + \_\_\_\_ = \_\_\_\_$ $\_\_\_\_ - \_\_\_\_ = \_\_\_\_$ $\_\_\_\_ - \_\_\_\_ = \_\_\_\_$	**b.** $\quad 6 \; + \_\_\_\_ = \; 9$ $\_\_\_\_ + \_\_\_\_ = \_\_\_\_$ $\_\_\_\_ - \_\_\_\_ = \_\_\_\_$ $\_\_\_\_ - \_\_\_\_ = \_\_\_\_$

4. Skip-count by tens.

   a. 4, 14, _____, _____, _____, _____, _____, _____

   b. _____, _____, _____, 68, 78, _____, _____, _____

5. **a.** Skip-count by fives starting at 45, and color all those numbers yellow.

   b. Skip-count by twos starting at 42, and color those numbers blue.

41	42	43	44	45	46	47	48	49	50
51	52	53	54	55	56	57	58	59	60
61	62	63	64	65	66	67	68	69	70

   Which numbers end up green?

6. Name and write the numbers.

   a. 1 ten 1 one _____

   b. 1 ten 7 ones _____

   c. 1 ten 5 ones _____

   d. 1 ten 3 ones _____

7. Find the difference between the numbers. "Travel" on the number line!

From	2	11	9	14	6	12	6	10
To	10	7	9	7	6	5	12	15
Difference								

8. Write < or > or = .

   a. 82 ☐ 29   **c.** 70 + 4 ☐ 7 + 40   **e.** 60 + 7 ☐ 70 + 5

   b. 75 ☐ 67   **d.** 20 + 8 ☐ 2 + 80   **f.** 2 + 90 ☐ 9 + 50

9. Solve.

   a. Some children needed 10 players for a game. They already had 2 boys and 2 girls. How many more children do they need for their game?

   b. A herd has 10 brown horses, 20 white horses, and 10 speckled ones. How many horses are there in the herd?

   How many more white horses are there than brown ones?

Addition and Subtraction Facts Review 1

1. Practice addition and subtraction facts with 6, 7, and 8.

a.	b.	c.	d.
0 + _____ = 8	3 + _____ = 7	6 − _____ = 2	7 − _____ = 2
3 + _____ = 8	5 + _____ = 7	6 − _____ = 5	8 − _____ = 3
2 + _____ = 8	1 + _____ = 7	6 − _____ = 3	6 − _____ = 1
6 + _____ = 8	6 + _____ = 7	6 − _____ = 4	8 − _____ = 4
5 + _____ = 8	2 + _____ = 7	6 − _____ = 1	7 − _____ = 4

2. First add and subtract. Write the answers below (not in the box!). Then compare, and write < , > or = .

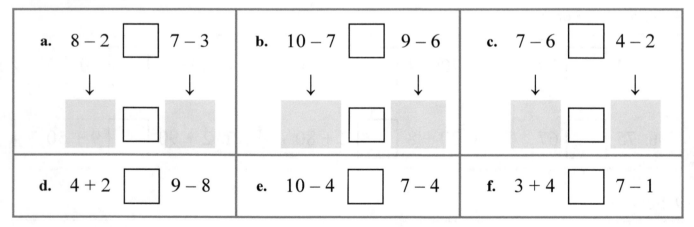

a.	8 − 2 ☐ 7 − 3	b.	10 − 7 ☐ 9 − 6	c.	7 − 6 ☐ 4 − 2
d.	4 + 2 ☐ 9 − 8	e.	10 − 4 ☐ 7 − 4	f.	3 + 4 ☐ 7 − 1

3. Solve.

a. Luisa and Caleb were playing a game. Luisa had 9 game pieces and Caleb had 4. How many more game pieces did Luisa have than Caleb?

b. Luisa gave one game piece to Caleb. Now, who has more game pieces?

How many more?

4. Complete. Then draw a line to connect the facts from the same fact family.

_____ − 5 = 1

2 + _____ = 7

8 − _____ = 3

_____ + 2 = 8

6 − 4 = _____

7 − 5 = _____

_____ + 2 = 6

6 − 1 = _____

5 + _____ = 8

8 − _____ = 6

8 − 3 = _____

5 + _____ = 7

1 + 5 = _____

8 − 6 = _____

2 + 4 = _____

5. Complete. Then draw a line to connect the facts from the same fact family.

3 + _____ = 7

6 − _____ = 3

_____ + 1 = 8

_____ − 4 = 4

7 − 1 = _____

_____ + 6 = 7

_____ − 7 = 1

3 + 3 = _____

4 + _____ = 7

8 − _____ = 4

8 − _____ = 7

1 + 6 = _____

3 + _____ = 6

8 − 4 = _____

7 − _____ = 4

Puzzle Corner

What numbers can go into the squares?
All the numbers are less than 10. Guess and check!

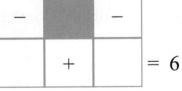

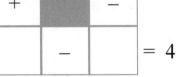

Addition and Subtraction Facts Review 2

1. Practice addition and subtraction facts with 9 and 10.

a.

4 + _____ = 9

1 + _____ = 9

6 + _____ = 9

2 + _____ = 9

b.

5 + _____ = 10

2 + _____ = 10

3 + _____ = 10

4 + _____ = 10

c.

10 – _____ = 1

10 – _____ = 7

10 – _____ = 5

10 – _____ = 8

d.

9 – _____ = 2

9 – _____ = 6

9 – _____ = 8

9 – _____ = 5

2. Match the addition problems to the right pictures and solve them.

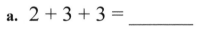
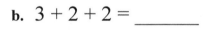
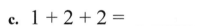

a. 2 + 3 + 3 = _____

b. 3 + 2 + 2 = _____

c. 1 + 2 + 2 = _____

d. 3 + 4 + 2 = _____

e. 3 + 3 + 3 = _____

f. 2 + 2 + 2 = _____

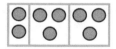

3. Ann, Joe, and Bill solved some problems again! Correct the ones that are wrong.

Ann:

a. 5 – 0 = △5

b. 10 – △3 = 6

Joe:

c. 9 – 4 = △6

d. 6 – △4 = 2

Bill:

e. 7 – △5 = 3

f. △8 – 6 = 2

4. Fill in the missing numbers. Draw a line to connect the facts that are from
   the same fact family.

$9 -$ _____ $= 7$

$9 -$ _____ $= 6$

$9 - 1 =$ _____

$9 -$ _____ $= 4$

_____ $+ 2 = 9$

$8 +$ _____ $= 9$

_____ $+ 5 = 9$

$3 +$ _____ $= 9$

$9 -$ _____ $= 5$

$9 - 6 =$ _____

$9 -$ _____ $= 2$

_____ $+ 8 = 9$

5. a. Draw a line to connect each pair of
      numbers that add up to 9.
      Which number is left by itself?

   b. Draw a line to connect each pair of
      numbers that add up to 10.
      Which number is left by itself?

0		7		2	
	2		8		5
1		6			
	9		4	3	4
		5			
	1			3	8
7			6		9

3		7	10	
	2		8	9
1		6		
	9		4	0	2
		5		
	1		3	8
7		6		5

6. Fill in the missing numbers. Draw a line to connect the facts that are from
   the same fact family.

$10 -$ _____ $= 8$

$10 -$ _____ $= 5$

$10 -$ _____ $= 1$

$10 - 3 =$ _____

$10 - 6 =$ _____

_____ $+ 9 = 10$

$4 +$ _____ $= 10$

$5 +$ _____ $= 10$

$2 +$ _____ $= 10$

_____ $+ 7 = 10$

_____ $+ 1 = 10$

$10 - 5 =$ _____

$10 - 4 =$ _____

_____ $+ 3 = 10$

$10 -$ _____ $= 8$

7. Solve.

a. Millie has two boxes of crayons. Ken has seven boxes.
How many more boxes does he have than she has?

b. Mike has three yellow toy cars, four blue cars, and
three red cars. How many cars does he have in total?

c. There were four birds in a tree. Four more flew in.
How many birds are there now?

Later, five of them flew away.
How many birds are there now?

d. Elisa knows she has ten crayons. She can only find four.
How many are missing?

e. A ten-piece puzzle has two pieces missing.
How many pieces are there now?

Addition and Subtraction Facts Test

1. Find the missing numbers.

a. 2 + _____ = 8	b. 2 + _____ = 9	c. 2 + _____ = 10
3 + _____ = 8	3 + _____ = 9	3 + _____ = 10
1 + _____ = 8	5 + _____ = 9	6 + _____ = 10
4 + _____ = 8	1 + _____ = 9	1 + _____ = 10

d.	e.	f.	g.
8 − 5 = _____	9 − 8 = _____	10 − 4 = _____	7 − 3 = _____
8 − 7 = _____	9 − 9 = _____	10 − 9 = _____	6 − 5 = _____
8 − 2 = _____	9 − 7 = _____	10 − 7 = _____	7 − 6 = _____
8 − 3 = _____	9 − 4 = _____	10 − 8 = _____	6 − 3 = _____

2. a. Sally has seven coins. Liz has three coins. Today, Liz found five more coins.
Now who has more coins?
How many more?

2. b. Dan had two boxes of nails. Then he bought four more boxes of nails.
The next day he gave three boxes to the neighbor.
How many boxes of nails does Dan have now?

3. a. Complete. Then connect with a line the facts from the same fact family.

_____ − 4 = 3	8 − 3 = _____
3 + _____ = 5	_____ + 3 = 7
8 − _____ = 5	5 − 2 = _____

b. Complete. Then connect with a line the facts from the same fact family.

2 + _____ = 6	_____ − 4 = 3
7 − _____ = 4	_____ − 6 = 3
_____ + 3 = 9	2 + 4 = _____

Mixed Review 3

1. Pick a number so the comparison is true.

3 4 5	4 5 6	3 4 5
2 + _____ < 6	1 + _____ > 6	4 + _____ < 8

2. Add.

   a. 0 + 4 + 2 = _____   **b.** 7 + 1 + 1 = _____   **c.** 2 + 5 + 3 = _____

3. Fill in the numbers and name them.

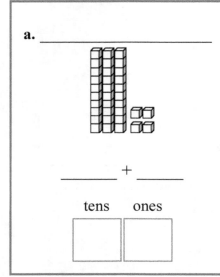

a. _____

_____ + _____

tens   ones

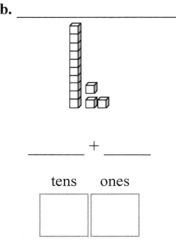

b. _____

_____ + _____

tens   ones

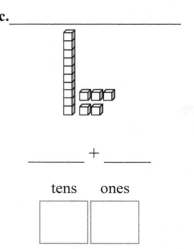

c. _____

_____ + _____

tens   ones

4. The numbers are broken into tens and ones. Fill in the missing parts.

a. 40 + _____ = 48	**b.** _____ + _____ = 62	**c.** 50 + 5 = _____

5. What number is...

a.	**b.**	**c.**
one more than 16 _____	two more than 11 _____	ten more than 12 _____
one less than 29 _____	two less than 67 _____	ten less than 30 _____
one less than 40 _____	two more than 59 _____	ten more than 87 _____

6. Count. You can also do this orally with your teacher.

96, 97, _____, _____, _____, _____, _____,

_____, _____, _____, _____, _____, _____

7. Draw tally marks for these numbers.

a. 9	**b.** 11
c. 27	**d.** 32

8. Some children counted how many stuffed animals they had.

a. How many does Alice have?

b. How many does Aaron have?

c. How many does Maria have?

d. Alice gave 10 stuffed animals to Aaron. Now how many does Alice have?

And Aaron?

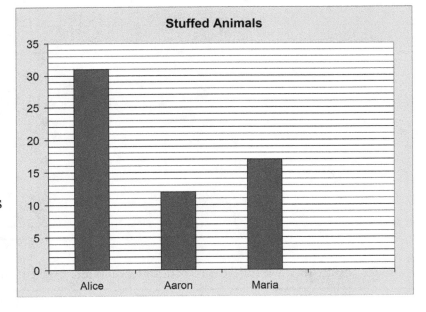

In the empty space you can draw a bar on the graph for how many stuffed animals you have.

9. Find the "mystery numbers"! You will need to think logically.

a. This number has three more tens than 50 has, and the same amount of ones as 13.	**b.** This number has seven less ones than 29, and six more tens than 17.

27

Clock Review

1. Write the time using the expressions *o'clock* or *half past*.

a. _____

b. _____

c. _____

d. _____

_____

_____

_____

_____

2. Write the time using numbers.

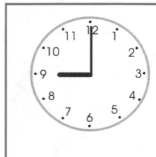   

a. _____ : _____

b. _____ : _____

c. _____ : _____

d. _____ : _____

3. Write the time for a half-hour and an hour later. Use numbers.

Now it is:	a. 5:00	b. 10:30	c. 12:00	d. 1:30	e. 5:30
A half-hour later, it is:					
An hour later, it is:					

4. Fill in either AM or PM.

a. Jack wakes up. It is 8 _____.	**b.** Jack plays in the afternoon. It is 3 _____.
c. Jack is sleeping. It is dark. It is 2 _____.	**d.** Time for an evening snack! It is 8 _____.

Clock Test

1. Write the time using the expressions *o'clock* and *half past*.

a. _____

_____

b. _____

_____

c. _____

_____

d. _____

_____

2. Write the time in two ways: using *o'clock* or *half past*, and with numbers.

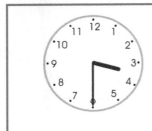

a. _____

_____

_____ : _____

b. _____

_____

_____ : _____

c. _____

_____

_____ : _____

d. _____

_____

_____ : _____

3. Write the time for a half-hour and an hour later from the given time. Use numbers.

Now it is:	a. 6:00	b. 9:30	c. 10:00	d. 4:30	e. 12:30
a half-hour later, it is:					
an hour later, it is:					

4. Fill in either AM or PM.

a. Anna wakes up. It is 7 _____.

b. Anna plays in the afternoon. It is 3 _____.

c. Anna sleeps. It is dark. It is 3 _____.

d. Time for an evening snack! It is 7 _____.

Mixed Review 4

1. Add.

a. $1 + 4 =$ _____	**b.** $5 + 2 =$ _____	**c.** $3 + 6 =$ _____	**d.** $7 + 3 =$ _____

2. Subtract.

a. $5 - 2 =$ _____   **b.** $9 - 4 =$ _____   **c.** $7 - 3 =$ _____   **d.** $10 - 8 =$ _____

e. $6 - 2 =$ _____   **f.** $10 - 7 =$ _____   **g.** $7 - 7 =$ _____   **h.** $9 - 5 =$ _____

3. Write the names of the numbers with whole tens.

two tens _____

three tens _____

eight tens _____

five tens _____

4. Put the numbers in order from the smallest to the largest.

a. 58, 17, 36	**b.** 23, 63, 36	**c.** 48, 84, 44
_____ < _____ < _____	_____ < _____ < _____	_____ < _____ < _____

5. Solve the missing numbers.

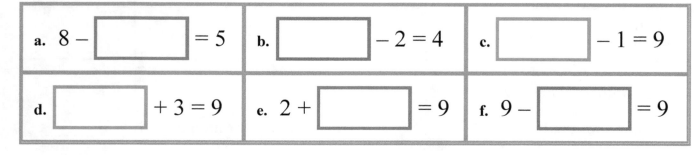

a. $8 - \boxed{} = 5$	**b.** $\boxed{} - 2 = 4$	**c.** $\boxed{} - 1 = 9$
d. $\boxed{} + 3 = 9$	**e.** $2 + \boxed{} = 9$	**f.** $9 - \boxed{} = 9$

6. Draw the hour hand on the clocks. Then write the time that the clock will show a half-hour later.

	a. two o'clock	b. ten o'clock	c. half-past six	d. half-past eight
1/2 hour later →	_____	_____	_____	_____

7. Fill in either AM or PM.

a. You woke up. It was 7 _____.	b. Jon plays in the afternoon at 3 _____.
c. Joe is asleep. It is dark. It is 1 _____.	d. It is time for lunch. It is 1 _____.

8. Compare. Write < , > , or = .

a. 62 ☐ 3 + 60	c. 10 − 2 ☐ 7	e. 7 ☐ 9 − 2
b. 54 ☐ 42 + 10	d. 6 − 5 ☐ 0	f. 45 ☐ 65 − 10

9. Solve.

a. A baby put some of his ten crayons into a bucket. Then he had 4 crayons on the floor. So, how many did he put into the bucket?

b. Theresa has $10. She gets another $4 from her mom. Now how much does she have?

How much more does she need to buy a $20 shirt?

Shapes and Measuring Review

1. Divide the shapes using one straight line.

    Divide the shape A into a triangle and a five-sided shape.

    Divide the shape B into a square and a rectangle.

    Divide the shape C into a four-sided shape and a triangle.

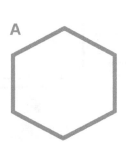

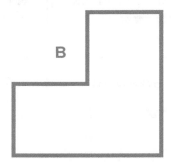

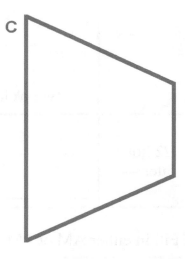

2. Color the triangles orange,
    the rectangles red,
    the squares blue, and
    the little circles light blue.

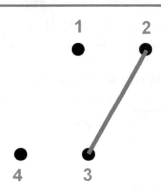

3. Join these dots <u>carefully</u> with lines, from 1 to 2 to 3 to 4 to 1. Use a ruler.

    What shape do you get?

    Divide your shape into two triangles.

4. How many corners are in this shape?

    (We call it a *pentagon*.)

    Measure its sides in centimeters.

Shapes and Measuring Test

1. The two shapes are put together.
   What new shape is formed?

   a. _____

   b. _____

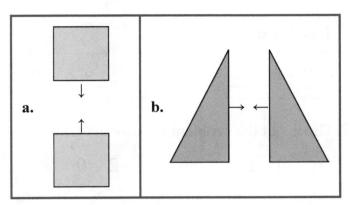

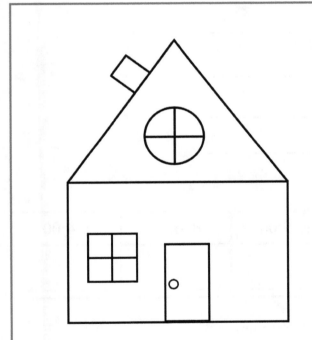

2. Color the triangle red, one rectangle
   green and the other purple,
   the squares yellow, and
   the circles light blue.

3. Join these dots <u>carefully</u> with lines.
   Use a ruler. What shape do you get?

   _____

   Measure the sides of your shape
   in inches.

4. Draw a line that is:

   a. 4 inches

   b. 12 centimeters

Mixed Review 5

1. Find the missing numbers.

a. $7 + \rule{1.5cm}{0.4pt} = 7$	b. $\rule{1.5cm}{0.4pt} + 6 = 9$	c. $4 + \rule{1.5cm}{0.4pt} = 9$	d. $8 + \rule{1.5cm}{0.4pt} = 10$

2. Cross out the problem if you can't take away that many.

$$4 - 6 \qquad\qquad 2 - 0 \qquad\qquad 6 - 9 \qquad\qquad 8 - 4$$

3. Write these numbers with words. You can also do this orally with your teacher.

a. 2 tens 9 ones = _____

b. 9 tens 1 one = _____

c. 1 ten 5 ones = _____

d. 5 tens 7 ones = _____

4. Write the time for a half-hour later. Use numbers.

Now it is:	a. 1:00	b. 11:30	c. 9:00	d. 6:30	e. 4:00
a half-hour later, it is:	___ : ___	___ : ___	___ : ___	___ : ___	___ : ___

5. Draw different shapes that you have learned, and label them.

6. Color the circles yellow,
   the triangles blue,
   the squares pink,
   the rectangles green
   and the rest of the shapes red.

7. Solve.

9 − ____ = 4	3 + ____ = 7	10 − ____ = 8
3 + ____ = 4	8 − ____ = 7	3 + ____ = 8
10 − ____ = 4	0 + ____ = 7	9 − ____ = 8
2 + ____ = 4	9 − ____ = 7	2 + ____ = 8

9 − ____ = 6	3 + ____ = 5	10 − ____ = 3
3 + ____ = 6	10 − ____ = 5	3 + ____ = 3
10 − ____ = 6	0 + ____ = 5	7 − ____ = 3
2 + ____ = 6	9 − ____ = 5	2 + ____ = 3

8. Write < or > between the numbers to compare them.

a. 30 < 38   b. 87   85   c. 69   96   d. 58   56

e. 60   48   f. 43   95   g. 49   94   h. 22   32

35

Adding and Subtracting Within 0-100 Review

1. Solve. Write the letter after each problem in the box below the right answer.

60 + ____ = 68 A	90 – 60 = _____ D	52 + ____ = 58 L
52 + ____ = 55 U	60 – 8 = _____ T	24 + ____ = 26 H
22 + ____ = 27 O	91 – 20 = _____ M	55 + ____ = 56 O
43 + ____ = 50 O	32 – 10 = _____ N	11 + ____ = 20 U
56 – 6 = _____ E 80 – 20 = _____ L	82 – 10 = _____ F 100 – 4 = _____ Y	88 – 10 = _____ F

96   7   9   72   1   3   22   30   8   6   60   5   78   52   2   50   71

☐☐☐   ☐☐☐☐☐   ☐☐☐   ☐☐   ☐☐☐☐ !

2. Write the numbers under each other in the boxes and add or subtract.

a. 31 + 45   **b.** 70 + 19   **c.** 26 + 73   **d.** 31 + 8

e. 77 – 22   **f.** 56 – 14   **g.** 99 – 45   **h.** 47 – 5

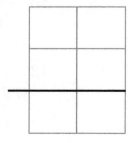 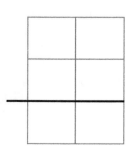 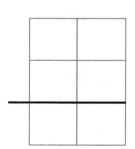 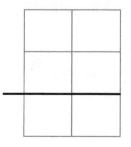

3. **a.** Fill in the doubles chart:

   b. Use the doubles chart to help you solve these
   addition problems. *Explain* how it helps you!

   5 + 5 = _____

   6 + 6 = _____

   7 + 8 = _____   6 + 7 = _____   7 + 7 = _____

   6 + 5 = _____   8 + 9 = _____   8 + 8 = _____

   9 + 9 = _____

4. Add. Tell which idea you use to add.

Trick with nine	**a.** 9 + 9 = _____	**b.** 8 + 4 = _____	Doubles chart
Trick with eight	**c.** 9 + 5 = _____	**d.** 7 + 7 = _____	Just one more than a double
"Just one more" than a sum with 10	**e.** 7 + 8 = _____	**f.** 6 + 5 = _____	I just know it!
	g. 3 + 9 = _____	**h.** 6 + 7 = _____	

5. Subtract.

a.

11 − 2 = _____
11 − 4 = _____
11 − 5 = _____
11 − 6 = _____

b.
12 − 4 = _____
12 − 5 = _____
12 − 3 = _____
12 − 6 = _____

c.
13 − 5 = _____
13 − 6 = _____
13 − 4 = _____
13 − 7 = _____

d.
14 − 5 = _____
14 − 8 = _____
14 − 7 = _____
14 − 6 = _____

e.
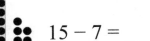
15 − 6 = _____
15 − 9 = _____
15 − 7 = _____
15 − 8 = _____

f.
16 − 8 = _____
16 − 9 = _____
16 − 7 = _____
16 − 6 = _____

6. One book in the pictogram means that the child read <u>5 books</u>.

a. How many books did
Mariana read?

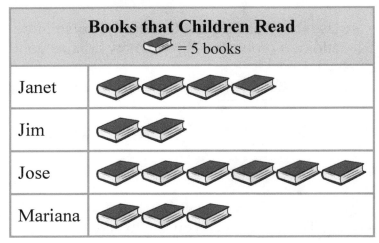

Books that Children Read

= 5 books

Janet	
Jim	
Jose	
Mariana	

b. How many books did
Jose read?

c. How many more books did
Janet read than Jim?

d. How many more books did Jose read than Janet?

e. Make your own question about the pictogram, and answer it!

7. Solve the word problems. Write number sentences for them.

a. Twenty birds were in a tree. Then, two flew away. Then, five flew away. How many are left?
b. Jack had five books. Then his mom gave him one more, and dad gave him three more. How many books does Jack have now?
c. Your sister is on page 14 of a 20-page book. How many pages does she have left to read?
d. How many years older is Sam than Jack, if Sam is 12 years old and Jack is 4?
e. Can you buy a $15 train if you first have $11 and then Mom gives you $5?

8. Add. In some of these problems you need to make a new ten with some of the little dots. You can also use the abacus.

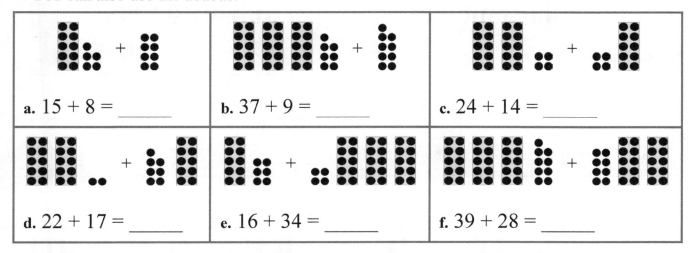

a. 15 + 8 = _____

b. 37 + 9 = _____

c. 24 + 14 = _____

d. 22 + 17 = _____

e. 16 + 34 = _____

f. 39 + 28 = _____

9. Pyramid numbers. Add two numbers that are next to each other, and put the sum *below* them both, in the middle.

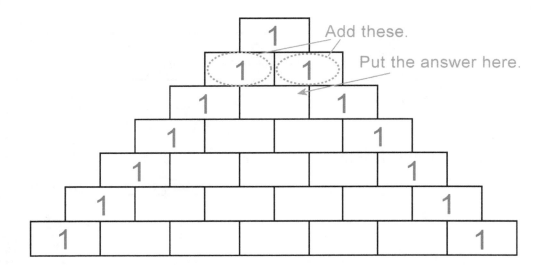

Add these.

Put the answer here.

Puzzle Corner   Find what was subtracted!

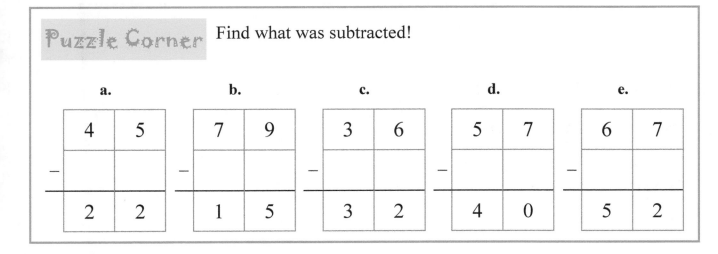

a.		b.		c.		d.		e.	
4	5	7	9	3	6	5	7	6	7
−		−		−		−		−	
2	2	1	5	3	2	4	0	5	2

Adding and Subtracting Within 0-100 Test

1. Add and subtract.

a. 22 + 4 = _____	**b.** 40 + 30 = _____	**c.** 90 − 20 = _____
41 + 5 = _____	76 + 10 = _____	80 − 70 = _____

2. Add. First, make a new ten with some of the little dots.

 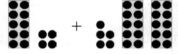 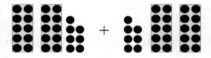

a. 25 + 38 = _____	**b.** 14 + 25 = _____	**c.** 27 + 27 = _____

3. Add. You can use the trick with nine and the trick with eight.

a. 9 + 9 = _____	**b.** 4 + 9 = _____	**c.** 8 + 5 = _____	**d.** 8 + 7 = _____

4. Add and subtract. Write the numbers under each other.

    a. 20 + 57   **b.** 78 − 44   **c.** 45 + 13   **d.** 87 − 20

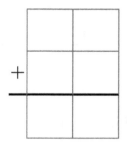 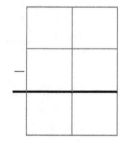

5. Jake had 6 dollars and Jim had 12. Then, Jake got 10 dollars more.

Now who has more money?

How many dollars more?

Mixed Review 6

1. Write the time using numbers.

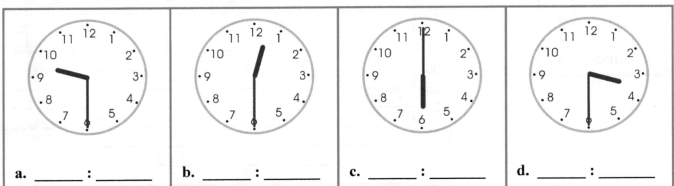

a. _____ : _____ b. _____ : _____ c. _____ : _____ d. _____ : _____

2. Write the time for a half-hour later. Use numbers.

Now it is:	a. 2:00	b. 8:00	c. 12:00	d. 7:30	e. 10:30
A half-hour later, it is:					

3. Continue the patterns.

a.	b.	c.
100 – 1 = _____	10 – 1 = _____	10 + 90 = _____
90 – 2 = _____	20 – 2 = _____	20 + 80 = _____
80 – 3 = _____	30 – 3 = _____	30 + 70 = _____
____ – ____ = ____	____ – ____ = ____	____ + ____ = ____
____ – ____ = ____	____ – ____ = ____	____ + ____ = ____
____ – ____ = ____	____ – ____ = ____	____ + ____ = ____
____ – ____ = ____	____ – ____ = ____	____ + ____ = ____
____ – ____ = ____	____ – ____ = ____	____ + ____ = ____

4. Some children played a board game. These are their point counts. Draw a bar graph.

Jeff	30
Santiago	45
Maria	20
Elizabeth	35

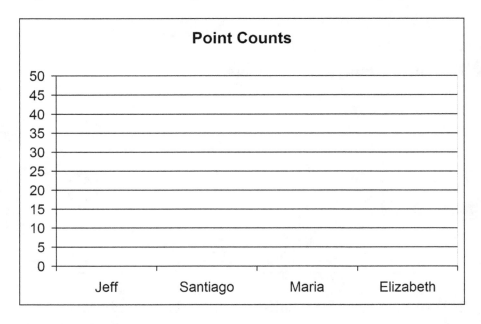

a. How many more points did Jeff get than Maria?

b. How many more points did Santiago get than Elizabeth?

5. Measure four things that are at most 12 inches long. Then make a bar graph about the length of those four things.

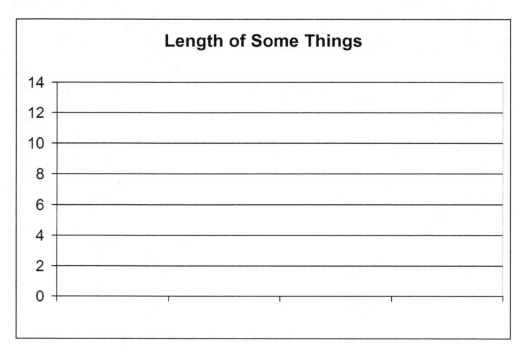

6. Draw here some dots and connect them with lines so that you get a _triangle_.

7. Divide these shapes by drawing a straight line or lines from dot to dot. Then color as you are asked.

a.	b.	c.	d.
Color one half.	Color one fourth.	Color two halves.	Color three fourths.

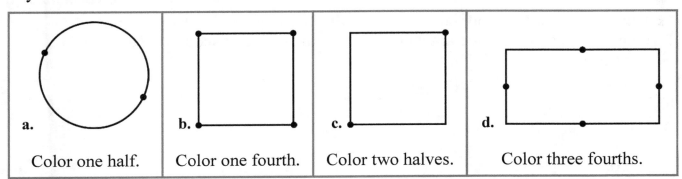

Puzzle Corner — Add the same number each time.

+ 2

8	_1 0_
18	___
38	___
68	___
98	___

+ 3

9	___
19	___
59	___
69	___
89	___

+ 4

7	___
17	___
47	___
77	___
97	___

Mixed Review 7

1. Find the missing numbers.

a.	b.	c.	d.
2 + _____ = 4	2 + _____ = 7	6 − _____ = 6	3 − 1 = _____
5 + _____ = 9	0 + _____ = 5	8 − _____ = 4	10 − 3 = _____

2. Find the "mystery numbers"! You will need to think logically.

a. This number has one more ten than 20 has, and the same amount of ones as 63.	**b.** This number has two less ones than 88, and six more tens than 24.

3. Count by tens.

   16, 26, _____, _____, _____, _____, _____, _____

4. Find how much the two items cost together.

a. a rabbit, $12, and a parrot, $65 Together they cost $ _____ .	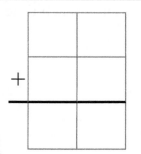	**b.** a bicycle, $76, and a flashlight, $23 Together they cost $ _____ .	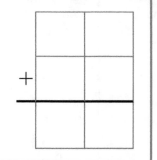

5. Draw the hands to show the time.

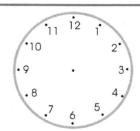	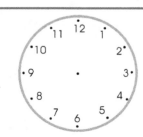	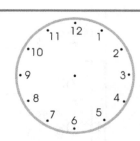	
a. 5 o'clock	**b.** half past seven	**c.** 11 o'clock	**d.** half past two

6. Fill in the blanks.

   a. _____ has four sides the same length.

   b. _____ has three sides and three vertices.

7. Add using the nine trick and the eight trick.

| **a.** $9 + 8 =$ _____ | **b.** $9 + 3 =$ _____ | **c.** $9 + 5 =$ _____ |
| $8 + 8 =$ _____ | $8 + 4 =$ _____ | $7 + 8 =$ _____ |

8. Subtract and add whole tens.

| **a.** $25 + 10 =$ _____ | **b.** $90 - 30 =$ _____ | **c.** $92 - 10 =$ _____ |
| $60 + 20 =$ _____ | $100 - 70 =$ _____ | $64 - 10 =$ _____ |

9. Divide these shapes by drawing straight lines from dot to dot. Then color.

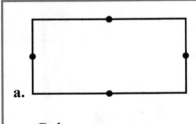 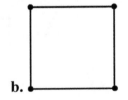 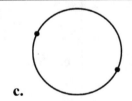 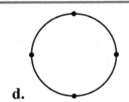

| **a.** Color one quarter. | **b.** Color two quarters. | **c.** Color two halves. | **d.** Color three fourths. |

10. Which is more, two quarters or one half?
    Coloring the parts in the pictures may help.

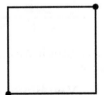 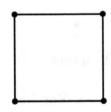

11. Name the basic shape. Is it a cylinder, a cube, a box, or a ball?

a.   **b.**   **c.**   **d.**

Coins Review

1. How much money? Write down the amount in cents.

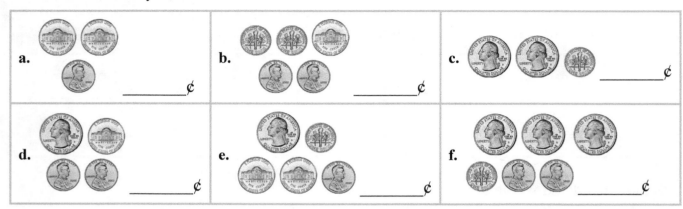

2. Draw coins to illustrate these amounts of money.

a. 52¢	**b.** 27¢	**c.** 76¢
d. 85¢	**e.** 79¢	**f.** 34¢

3. You buy an item. How much money will you have left?

a. You have:	You buy a comb for 29¢. How much is left?	**b.** You have:	You buy hairpins for 62¢. How much is left?

Coins Test

1. How much money? Write the amount in cents.

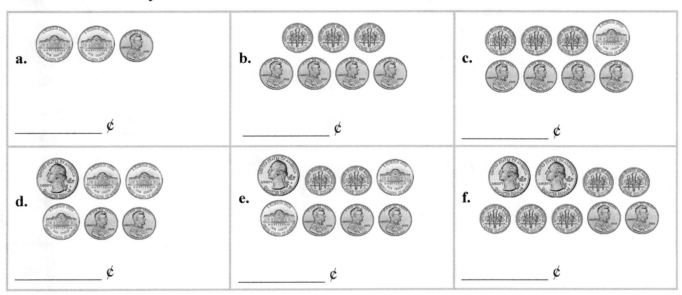

2. Draw to make these amounts of money.

a. 63¢	b. 38¢	c. 69¢

3. You buy an item. How much money will you have left?

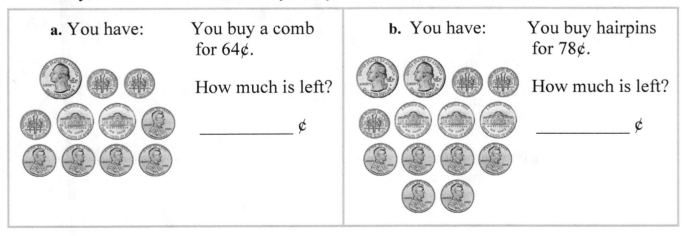

Mixed Review 8

1. Find the missing numbers.

a.	b.	c.	d.
_____ − 1 = 9	8 + 9 = _____	25 − 10 = _____	52 + 7 = _____
_____ − 2 = 6	7 + 8 = _____	38 − 10 = _____	35 + 3 = _____
_____ − 3 = 4	5 + 6 = _____	100 − 10 = _____	26 + 2 = _____

2. Draw the hour hand.

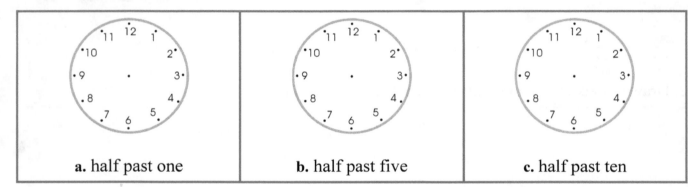

a. half past one   b. half past five   c. half past ten

3. Trace and cut the shapes to do the exercises, or
   if you can, imagine putting the shapes together,
   and sketch (draw) the answer shapes.

   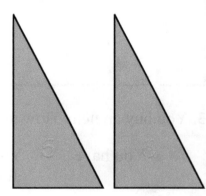

   a. Put together the #5 triangles so that you get
      a rectangle.

   b. Now place them together so that you get a
      different four-sided shape (not a rectangle).

   c. Use some of the #1 (yellow) triangles to form
      the purple shape (#6)

   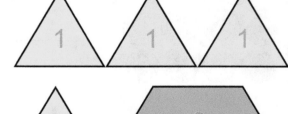

   d. Now use a #1 triangle and the purple shape.
      What shapes can you make with these two?

48

4. First subtract to 10. Then subtract the rest.

| a. 15 − 7
 / \
 15 − ___ − ___

 = ___ | b. 14 − 9
 / \
 14 − ___ − ___

 = ___ | c. 16 − 8
 / \
 16 − ___ − ___

 = ___ |

5. Add and subtract.

a.   2 5
    + 3 0

b.   5 1
    + 3 4

c   7 8
   − 1 5

d.   8 6
    − 4 4

6. Draw circles to make these amounts of money. Put **P** on pennies, **D** on dimes,
   N on nickels and **Q** on quarters. Use the least number of coins possible.

| a. 32¢ | b. 15¢ | c. 26¢ |
| d. 80¢ | e. 66¢ | f. 43¢ |

7. You bought an item. How much money do you have left?

| **a.** You have:  | You bought a bar of soap for 59¢.

 How much is left?

 _____ ¢ | **b.** You have:  | You bought a toy for 86¢.

 How much is left?

 _____ ¢ |

This page left blank intentionally.

Math Mammoth End-of-the-Year Test - Grade 1

This test is quite long, so I do not recommend that you have your child/student to do it in one sitting. Break it into parts and administer them either on consecutive days, or perhaps on morning/evening/morning. Use your judgment.

This is to be used as a diagnostic test. Thus, you may even skip those areas and concepts that you already know for sure your student has mastered.

The test does not cover every single concept that is covered in *Math Mammoth Grade 1*, but all of the major concepts and ideas are tested here. This test is evaluating the child's ability in the following content areas:

- basic addition and subtraction facts within 0-10
- two-digit numbers
- adding and subtracting two-digit numbers
- basic word problems
- clock to the nearest half hour
- measuring and geometry (shapes)
- counting coins

Note 1: If the child cannot read, the teacher can read the questions.

Note 2: Problems #1 and #2 are done <u>orally and timed</u>. Let the student see the problems. Read each problem aloud, and wait a maximum of 5 seconds for an answer. Mark the problem as right or wrong according to the student's (oral) answer. Mark it wrong if there is no answer. Then you can move on to the next problem.

You do not have to mention to the student that the problems are timed or that he/she will have 5 seconds per answer, because the idea here is not to create extra pressure by the fact it is timed, but simply to check if the student has the facts memorized (quick recall). You can say for example (vary as needed):

"I will ask you some addition and subtraction questions. Try to answer them as quickly as possible. In each question, I will only wait a little while for you to answer, and if you don't say anything, I will move on to the next problem. So just try your best to answer the questions as quickly as you can."

In order to continue with the Math Mammoth Grade 2, I recommend that the child gain a score of 80% on this test, and that the teacher or parent review with him any content areas that are found weak. Children scoring between 70 and 80% may also continue with grade 2, depending on the types of errors (careless errors or not remembering something, vs. lack of understanding). Again, use your judgment.

Grading

My suggestion for grading is below. The total is 108 points. A score of 86 points is 80%. A score of 76 points is 70%.

Question	Max. points	Student score
Basic Addition and Subtraction Facts within 0-10		
1	8 points	
2	8 points	
3	4 points	
4	8 points	
	subtotal	/ 28
Place Value and Two-Digit Numbers		
5	6 points	
6	4 points	
7	3 points	
	subtotal	/ 13
Adding and Subtracting Two-Digit Numbers		
8	6 points	
9	6 points	
10	4 points	
11	3 points	
	subtotal	/ 19

Question	Max. points	Student score
Basic Word Problems		
12	2 points	
13	2 points	
14	2 points	
15	2 points	
16	2 points	
17	6 points	
18	6 points	
	subtotal	/ 22
Clock		
19	6 points	
20	8 points	
	subtotal	/ 14
Geometry and Measuring		
21	2 points	
22	5 points	
	subtotal	/ 7
Money		
23	3 points	
24	2 points	
	subtotal	/ 5
	TOTAL	/ 108

End of the Year Test - Grade 1

Basic Addition and Subtraction Facts within 0-10

In problems 1 and 2, your teacher will read you the addition and subtraction questions. Try to answer them as quickly as possible. In each question, he/she will only wait a little while for you to answer, and if you don't say anything, your teacher will move on to the next problem. So, just try your best to answer the questions as quickly as you can.

1. Add.

a.	b.	c.	d.
$2 + 3 =$ _____	$7 + 3 =$ _____	$6 + 2 =$ _____	$5 + 5 =$ _____
$4 + 4 =$ _____	$5 + 4 =$ _____	$4 + 6 =$ _____	$2 + 4 =$ _____
$1 + 6 =$ _____	$3 + 6 =$ _____	$2 + 5 =$ _____	$9 + 1 =$ _____
$2 + 7 =$ _____	$1 + 7 =$ _____	$6 + 2 =$ _____	$5 + 3 =$ _____

2. Subtract.

a.	b.	c.	d.
$8 - 3 =$ _____	$5 - 3 =$ _____	$7 - 3 =$ _____	$10 - 3 =$ _____
$6 - 4 =$ _____	$7 - 4 =$ _____	$9 - 4 =$ _____	$5 - 4 =$ _____
$10 - 6 =$ _____	$9 - 6 =$ _____	$4 - 3 =$ _____	$8 - 6 =$ _____
$8 - 7 =$ _____	$6 - 3 =$ _____	$10 - 7 =$ _____	$9 - 7 =$ _____

3. Write a fact family to match the picture.

_____ + _____ = _____   _____ + _____ = _____

_____ − _____ = _____   _____ − _____ = _____

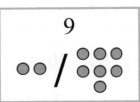

4. Find the missing numbers.

a. 2 + _____ = 7	**b.** 1 + _____ = 8	**c.** 4 + _____ = 6	**d.** _____ + 3 = 8
3 + _____ = 8	2 + _____ = 10	_____ + 3 = 9	_____ + 6 = 10

Place Value and Two-Digit Numbers

5. Fill in the missing parts.

a. 20 + 7 = _____	**b.** 6 + _____ = 56	**c.** 40 + _____ = 40
5 + 60 = _____	30 + _____ = 39	4 + _____ = 94

6. Put the numbers in order.

a. 16, 61, 26	**b.** 54, 14, 51
_____ < _____ < _____	_____ < _____ < _____

7. Compare the expressions and write $<$, $>$, or $=$.

    a. 40 + 8 ☐ 4 + 80   **b.** 43 + 5 ☐ 50   **c.** 3 + 33 ☐ 36

Adding and Subtracting Two-Digit Numbers

8. Add.

a. 84 + 4 = _____	**b.** 6 + 70 = _____	**c.** 74 + 5 = _____
41 + 4 = _____	16 + 2 = _____	6 + 53 = _____

9. Subtract.

a. 80 – 30 = _____	**b.** 55 – 3 = _____	**c.** 29 – 3 = _____
17 – 3 = _____	100 – 40 = _____	50 – 2 = _____

10. Add and subtract.

a.　　 1 4
　　　+ 3 5

b.　　 5 9
　　　－ 3 4

c.　　 4 0
　　　+ 5 6

d.　　 9 6
　　　－ 6 0

11. Add. The images can help you.

　　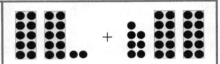

a. $19 + 34 =$ _____

b. $25 + 25 =$ _____

c. $22 + 27 =$ _____

Basic Word Problems

12. Write a subtraction sentence that matches with the addition $6 + 8 = 14$.

　　_____ $-$ _____ $=$ _____

13. How many more is 70 than 50?　　_____ more

14. Henry owns four more cars than Mark, and Mark owns six cars.
　　Draw Mark's cars and Henry's cars.

15. Ten kids are playing in the yard. There are 6 boys. How many girls are there?

16. Andy had 20 dollars. He bought a book for 10 dollars and another for 5 dollars.
　　How much money does he have left?

17. A parking lot has 30 spaces for cars. There is a car in 22 of those spaces.

   a. How many spaces are empty?

   b. Now, two more cars drive in. How many cars are now in the parking lot?

   c. How many empty spaces are there now?

18. Isabelle had 70 marbles and her sister had 55. Isabelle gave 10 marbles to her sister.

   a. Now how many marbles does Isabelle have?

   b. And her sister?

   c. Who has more? How many more?

Clock

19. Write the time in two ways: using *o'clock* or *half past*, and with numbers.

a.	b.	c.
_____	_____	_____
_____	_____	_____
_____ : _____	_____ : _____	_____ : _____

20. Write the time for a half-hour and an hour later from the given time. Use numbers.

Now it is:	**a.** 5:30	**b.** 7:00	**c.** 11:30	**d.** 12:00
a half-hour later, it is:				
an hour later, it is:				

21. Draw a line that is:

   a. 3 inches

   b. 9 centimeters

22. **a.** Join these dots carefully with a ruler so that you get a shape.

         A .   .B

         D ·   · C

   b. What is this shape called? _____

   c. Measure the sides of your shape in centimeters.

      Side AB: _____ cm   Side BC: _____ cm

   d. Draw a straight line from dot A to dot C. The line divides your shape to two new shapes.

      What are the new shapes called? _____

23. How much money? Write the amount in cents.

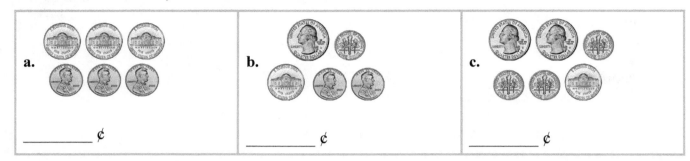

a. _____ ¢

b. _____ ¢

c. _____ ¢

24. Solve.

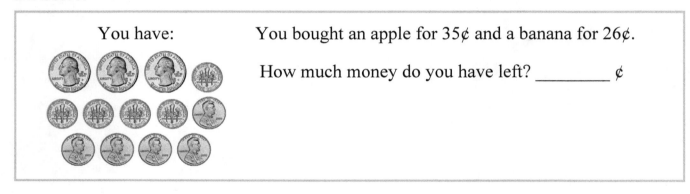

You have:

You bought an apple for 35¢ and a banana for 26¢.

How much money do you have left? _____ ¢

Math Mammoth Grade 1 Review Workbook Answers

Addition Within 0-10 Review, p. 5

1. Answers will vary.

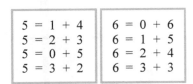

5 = 1 + 4	6 = 0 + 6
5 = 2 + 3	6 = 1 + 5
5 = 0 + 5	6 = 2 + 4
5 = 3 + 2	6 = 3 + 3

2.

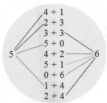

3.

4 + 2 = 6	6 + 0 = 6
2 + 3 = 5	0 + 5 = 5
1 + 4 = 5	3 + 3 = 6
6 + 0 = 6	4 + 2 = 6
5 + 1 = 6	1 + 4 = 5

4.

2 + 2 < 5	4 + 4 > 5	6 = 2 + 4
2 + 3 = 5	5 + 5 > 5	6 < 2 + 5
2 + 4 > 5	5 + 0 = 5	6 < 2 + 6

5.

7 = 0 + 7	8 = 0 + 8
7 = 1 + 6	8 = 1 + 7
7 = 2 + 5	8 = 2 + 6
7 = 3 + 4	8 = 3 + 5
7 = 4 + 3	8 = 4 + 4
7 = 5 + 2	8 = 5 + 3

6.

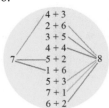

7.

5 + 2 = 7	4 + 4 = 8
3 + 4 = 7	3 + 4 = 7
2 + 6 = 8	3 + 5 = 8
5 + 3 = 8	7 + 1 = 8
6 + 1 = 7	5 + 2 = 7

8.

3 + 3 < 7	6 + 1 = 7	8 < 6 + 4
4 + 3 = 7	6 + 6 > 7	8 = 4 + 4
5 + 3 > 7	6 + 4 > 7	8 < 5 + 4

9. Answers will vary.

9 = 9 + 0	10 = 0 + 10
9 = 1 + 8	10 = 1 + 9
9 = 7 + 2	10 = 2 + 8
9 = 3 + 6	10 = 3 + 7
9 = 4 + 5	10 = 4 + 6
9 = 2 + 7	10 = 5 + 5

10.

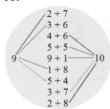

11.

8 + 2 = 10	3 + 6 = 9
5 + 4 = 9	7 + 3 = 10
2 + 7 = 9	3 + 6 = 9
5 + 5 = 10	7 + 2 = 9
6 + 4 = 10	4 + 6 = 10

12.

2 + 6 < 9	6 + 6 > 10	10 < 10 + 4
4 + 6 > 9	5 + 5 = 10	10 = 10 + 0
3 + 6 = 9	4 + 4 < 10	10 < 10 + 7

13.

a.	b.	c.
8 + 1 = 9	4 + 1 + 1 = 6	5 + 2 + 0 + 0 = 7
6 + 2 = 8	8 + 2 + 0 = 10	4 + 3 + 1 + 2 = 10
1 + 7 = 8	1 + 3 + 6 = 10	1 + 2 + 2 + 1 = 6
3 + 4 = 7	2 + 2 + 4 = 8	2 + 3 + 1 + 3 = 9

14.

+	2	4	3	6	7	5	8
1	3	5	4	7	8	6	9
3	5	7	6	9	10	8	11
4	6	8	7	10	11	9	12
2	4	6	5	8	9	7	10

Puzzle corner:

a. △ = 3 and □ = 5

b. □ = 5 and △ = 2

c. □ = 3 and △ = 2

Addition Within 0-10 Test, p. 9

1. a. 6   b. 9   c. 8   d. 10   e. 9   f. 9

2. a. <   b. <   c. <   d. =   e. >   f. >   g. <   h. =

3. a. 4 + 6 = 10   b. 3 + 4 = 7   c. 5 + 5 = 10

4. 5   b. 3   c. 6   d. 2

5. a. They have 10 stuffed animals. 7 + 3 = 10   b. Six pairs are not in the wash. 2 + 6 = 8 (or 8 − 2 = 6).

Subtraction Within 0-10 Review, p. 10

1. 2 + 7 = 9; 7 + 2 = 9; 9 − 2 = 7; 9 − 7 = 2

2. a. 10 − 4 = 6 or 10 − 6 = 4   b. 5 + 4 = 9; 9 − 5 = 4

3. a. 6 boys   b. 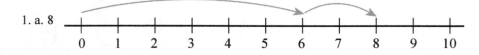   c. 2 more.

4. a. 1, 8, 7, 5   b. 3, 3, 1, 2   c. 10, 2, 0, 3   d. 6, 4, 9, 7

Subtraction Within 0-10 Test, p. 11

1. 2 + 6 = 8; 6 + 2 = 8; 8 − 2 = 6; 8 − 6 = 2

2. a. 9 − 5 = 4 or 9 − 4 = 5   b. 6 + 4 = 10; 10 − 6 = 4

3. a. There are 6 cats.   b.    c. There are 5 more robins than sparrows.

4. a. 2, 7, 5, 3   b. 6, 2, 7, 6   c. 9, 6, 2, 6   d. 1, 1, 0, 3

Mixed Review 1, p. 12

1. a. 8

b. 5

c. 4

2. a. 4 + 6 = 10   10 − 4 = 6
   b. 5 + 3 = 8   8 − 5 = 3

3. a. 7   b. 10   c. 4   d. 9   e. 7

4. a. 7   b. 6   c. 7

5. a. =   b. <   c. <   d. =   e. =   f. >

6. a. 10, 8   b. 9, 8   c. 7, 5   d. 7, 5

7.

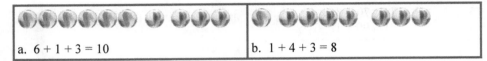

a. $6 + 1 + 3 = 10$ b. $1 + 4 + 3 = 8$

8.

a. Numbers: 9, 5, 4	b. Numbers: 10, 2, 8
$5 + 4 = 9$	$2 + 8 = 10$
$4 + 5 = 9$	$8 + 2 = 10$
$9 - 5 = 4$	$10 - 2 = 8$
$9 - 4 = 5$	$10 - 8 = 2$

9.

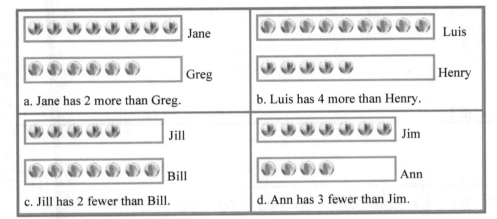

Jane

Greg

a. Jane has 2 more than Greg.

Luis

Henry

b. Luis has 4 more than Henry.

Jill

Bill

c. Jill has 2 fewer than Bill.

Jim

Ann

d. Ann has 3 fewer than Jim.

10. a. $3 + 5 - 1 = 7$ children
    b. $3 + 7 = 10$ marbles together; $7 - 3 = 4$ more than Judy
    c. $10 - 7 = 3$ blue trucks
    d. $9 - 6 = 3$ more dollars
    e. $3 + 5 = 8$ socks. Matt found $10 - 8 = 2$ socks still missing

Place Value Within 0-100 Review, p. 15

1. a. 1 ten 5 ones   _15_   fifteen
   b. 6 tens 7 ones   67   sixty-seven
   c. 4 tens 0 ones   40   forty
   d. 10 tens 0 ones   100   hundred
   e. 5 tens 1 one   51   fifty-one

2.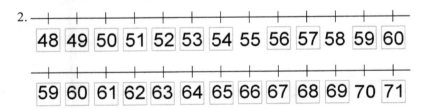

48 49 50 51 52 53 54 55 56 57 58 59 60

59 60 61 62 63 64 65 66 67 68 69 70 71

3. a. 87   b. 25   c. 57   d. 80   e. 101

4. 97, 98, 99, 100, 101, 102, 103,
   104, 105, 106, 107, 108, 109

Place Value Within 0-100 Review, cont.

5.

a. 45 = 40 + 5 68 = 60 + 8	b. 25 = 20 + 5 54 = 50 + 4	c. 78 = 70 + 8 91 = 90 + 1

6.

a. 50 + 7 = 57 20 + 0 = 20	b. 8 + 10 = 18 9 + 70 = 79	c. 90 + 6 = 96 9 + 60 = 69

7. a. 17 < 57 < 75   b. 18 < 41 < 44 < 48

8. a. 56 $<$ 5 + 60   b. 20 + 8 $<$ 33   c. 60 + 5 $>$ 50 + 6

   d. 34 $<$ 30 + 6   e. 4 + 90 $>$ 49   f. 80 + 2 $>$ 70 + 9

9. a. 13, 15, 17, 19, 21, 23, 25, 27, 29
   b. 18, 28, 38, 48, 58, 68, 78 , 88, 98
   c. 30, 35, 40, 45, 50, 55, 60, 65, 70

Mystery Number: 54

Place Value Within 0-100 Test, p. 17

1. a. sixteen   b. seventy-eight   c. fifty-one   d. ninety

2.

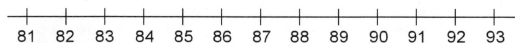

3. a. 86 = 80 + 6   b. 52 = 50 + 2, 32 = 30 + 2   c. 97 = 90 + 7, 19 = 10 + 9

4. a. 29   b. 75   c. 82   d. 91

5. a. 57 < 71 < 75   b. 69 < 96 < 98   c. 49 < 81 < 84

6. a. =   b. <   c. >

Mixed Review 2, p. 18

1. a. 22 = 20 + 2   b. 64 = 60+ 4   c. 95 = 90 + 5

2. a. <   b. =   c. >   d. <   e. =   f. =

3.

a. 3 + 7 = 10 7 + 3 = 10 10 − 7 = 3 10 − 3 = 7	b. 6 + 3 = 9 3 + 6 = 9 9 − 3 = 6 9 − 6 = 3

4. a. 4, 14, 24, 34, 44, 54, 64, 74
   b. 38, 48, 58, 68, 78, 88, 98, 108

Mixed Review 2, cont.

5. b. 50, 60 and 70 will be green if your blue and yellow blend together.

41	42	43	44	45	46	47	48	49	50
51	52	53	54	55	56	57	58	59	60
61	62	63	64	65	66	67	68	69	70

6. a. eleven   b. seventeen   c. fifteen   d. thirteen

7.

From	2	11	9	14	6	12	6	10
To	10	7	9	7	6	5	12	15
Difference	8	4	0	7	0	7	6	5

8. a. >   b. >   c. >   d. <   e. <   f. >

9. a. $10 - 2 - 2 = 6$. They need 6 more children.
  b. $10 + 20 + 10 = 40$ horses; $20 - 10 = 10$ more white than brown horses.

Addition and Subtraction Facts Review 1, p. 20

1.

a.	b.	c.	d.
$0 + 8 = 8$	$3 + 4 = 7$	$6 - 4 = 2$	$7 - 5 = 2$
$3 + 5 = 8$	$5 + 2 = 7$	$6 - 1 = 5$	$8 - 5 = 3$
$2 + 6 = 8$	$1 + 6 = 7$	$6 - 3 = 3$	$6 - 5 = 1$
$6 + 2 = 8$	$6 + 1 = 7$	$6 - 2 = 4$	$8 - 4 = 4$
$5 + 3 = 8$	$2 + 5 = 7$	$6 - 5 = 1$	$7 - 3 = 4$

2.

a. $8 - 2 \boxed{} 7 - 3$	b. $10 - 7 \boxed{} 9 - 6$	c. $7 - 6 \boxed{} 4 - 2$
$\downarrow \qquad \downarrow$	$\downarrow \qquad \downarrow$	$\downarrow \qquad \downarrow$
6 > 4	3 = 3	1 < 2
d. $4 + 2 > 9 - 8$	e. $10 - 4 > 7 - 4$	f. $3 + 4 > 7 - 1$

3. a. Luisa had 5 more counters. $9 - 4 = 5$ or $4 + 5 = 9$.   b. Luisa had three more counters. $8 - 5 = 3$ or $5 + 3 = 8$.

4.
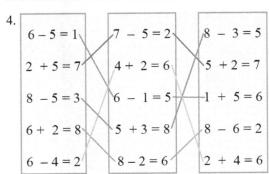

Addition and Subtraction Facts Review 1, cont.

5.

3 + 4 = 7	1 + 6 = 7	8 − 1 = 7
6 − 3 = 3	8 − 7 = 1	1 + 6 = 7
7 + 1 = 8	3 + 3 = 6	3 + 3 = 6
8 − 4 = 4	4 + 3 = 7	8 − 4 = 4
7 − 1 = 6	8 − 4 = 4	7 − 3 = 4

Puzzle Corner.
Answers vary.
These are just
example answers.

2	+	6	= 8
−		−	
2	+	4	= 6
=		=	
0		2	

3	+	4	= 7
+		−	
5	−	1	= 4
=		=	
8		3	

Addition and Subtraction Facts Review 2, p. 22

1.

a.	b.	c.	d.
4 + <u>5</u> = 9	5 + <u>5</u> = 10	10 − <u>9</u> = 1	9 − <u>7</u> = 2
1 + <u>8</u> = 9	2 + <u>8</u> = 10	10 − <u>3</u> = 7	9 − <u>3</u> = 6
6 + <u>3</u> = 9	3 + <u>7</u> = 10	10 − <u>5</u> = 5	9 − <u>1</u> = 8
2 + <u>7</u> = 9	4 + <u>6</u> = 10	10 − <u>2</u> = 8	9 − <u>4</u> = 5

2.

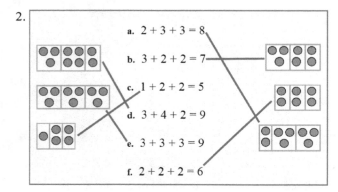

a. 2 + 3 + 3 = 8
b. 3 + 2 + 2 = 7
c. 1 + 2 + 2 = 5
d. 3 + 4 + 2 = 9
e. 3 + 3 + 3 = 9
f. 2 + 2 + 2 = 6

3. a. Correct.
   b. Should be 10 − <u>4</u> = 6.
   c. Should be 9 − 4 = <u>5</u>.
   d. Correct.
   e. Should be 7 − <u>4</u> = 3.
   f. Correct.

4.

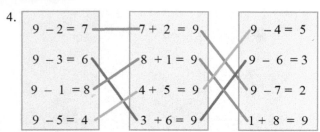

9 − 2 = 7	7 + 2 = 9	9 − 4 = 5
9 − 3 = 6	8 + 1 = 9	9 − 6 = 3
9 − 1 = 8	4 + 5 = 9	9 − 7 = 2
9 − 5 = 4	3 + 6 = 9	1 + 8 = 9

Addition and Subtraction Facts Review, cont.

5. a. One of the 9's is left by itself. b. One of the 6's is left by itself.

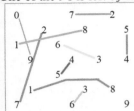 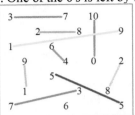

6.

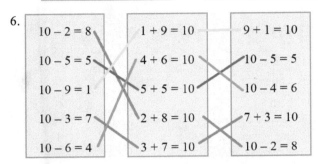

7. a. $7 - 2 = 5$. Ken has five more than Millie.
   b. $3 + 4 + 3 = 10$. Mike has ten cars.
   c. $4 + 4 = 8$. There were eight birds. $8 - 5 = 3$. Later, there were three birds.
   d. $4 + 6 = 10$ or $10 - 4 = 6$. Six crayons are missing.
   e. $10 - 2 = 8$. There are eight pieces left.

Addition and Subtraction Facts Test, p. 25

1. a. 6, 5, 7, 4   b. 7, 6, 4, 8   c. 8, 7, 4, 9   d. 3, 1, 6, 5   e. 1, 0, 2, 5   f. 6, 1, 3, 2   g. 4, 1, 1, 3

2. a. Liz now has $3 + 5 = 8$. So Liz has $8 - 7 = 1$ more.
   b. $2 + 4 = 6$ and $6 - 3 = 3$. So Dan now has 3 boxes of nails.

3. a.

$\underline{7} - 4 = 3$	$8 - 3 = \underline{5}$
$3 + \underline{2} = 5$	$\underline{4} + 3 = 7$
$8 - \underline{3} = 5$	$5 - 2 = \underline{3}$

b.

$2 + \underline{4} = 6$	$\underline{7} - 4 = 3$
$7 - \underline{3} = 4$	$\underline{9} - 6 = 3$
$\underline{6} + 3 = 9$	$2 + 4 = \underline{6}$

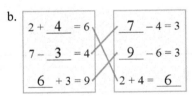

Mixed Review 3, p. 26

1.

2 + 3 < 6	1 + 6 > 6	4 + 3 < 8

2. a. 0 + 4 + 2 = 6   b. 7 + 1 + 1 = 9   c. 2 + 5 + 3 = 10

3.

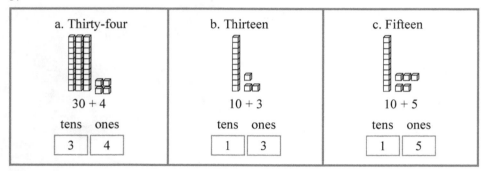

a. Thirty-four	b. Thirteen	c. Fifteen
30 + 4	10 + 3	10 + 5
tens ones	tens ones	tens ones
3 4	1 3	1 5

4.

a. 40 + _8_ = 48	b. 60 + _2_ = _62_	c. 50 + 5 = _55_

5. a. 17; 28; 39   b. 13; 65; 61   c. 22; 20; 97

6. 96, 97, 98 , 99 , 100 , 101 , 102 , 103 , 104 , 105 , 106, 107 , 108

7.

a. 9 卌 IIII	b. 11 卌 卌 I
c. 27 卌 卌 卌 卌 卌 II	d. 32 卌 卌 卌 卌 卌 卌 II

8. a. Alice has 31.   b. Aaron has 12.   c. Maria has 17.   d. Now Alice has 21 and Aaron has 22.

9. a. 83   b. 72

Clock Review, p. 28

1. a. half past 7   b. 2 o'clock   c. half past 12   d. half past 3

2. a. 9:00   b. 9:30   c. 4:30   d. 12:00

3. a. 5:30, 6:00   b. 11:00, 11:30   c. 12:30, 1:00   d. 2:00, 2:30   e. 6:00, 6:30

4. a. AM   b. PM   c. AM   d. PM

Clock Test, p. 29

1. a. 1 o'clock   b. half past 5   c. 7 o'clock   d. half past 12

2. a. half past 3 or 3:30   b. 9 o'clock or 9:00   c. half past 2 or 2:30   d. half past 11 or 11:30

3.

Now it is:	a. 6:00	b. 9:30	c. 10:00	d. 4:30	e. 12:30
a half-hour later, it is:	6:30	10:00	10:30	5:00	1:00
an hour later, it is:	7:00	10:30	11:00	5:30	1:30

4. a. AM   b. PM   c. AM   d. PM

Mixed Review 4, p. 30

1. a. 5   b. 7   c. 9   d. 10

2. a. $5 - 2 = 3$ b. $9 - 4 = 5$ c. $7 - 3 = 4$ d. $10 - 8 = 2$
   e. $6 - 2 = 4$ f. $10 - 7 = 3$ g. $7 - 7 = 0$ h. $9 - 5 = 4$

3. two tens   twenty
   three tens   thirty
   eight tens   eighty
   five tens   fifty

4. a. $17 < 36 < 58$ b. $23 < 36 < 63$ c. $44 < 48 < 84$

5. a. 3   b. 6   c. 10   d. 6   e. 7   f. 0

6.

	a. two o'clock	b. ten o'clock	c. half-past six	d. half-past eight
1/2 hour later →	half past two	half past ten	seven o'clock	nine o'clock

7. a. When you woke up. It was 7 <u>AM</u>.	b. Jon plays in the afternoon at 3 <u>PM</u>.
c. Joe is asleep. It is dark. It is 1 <u>AM</u>.	d. It is time for lunch. It is 1 <u>PM</u>.

8. a. <   b. >   c. >   d. >   e. =   f. <

9. a. $10 - 4 = 6$ crayons in the bucket.
   b. $10 + 4 = 14$ dollars. $14 + 6 = 20$ She needs six more dollars.

Shapes and Measuring Review, p. 32

1.

c: Answers can vary. For example:

2.

3.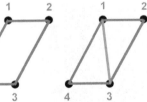

It is a quadrilateral (or, to be more precise, a parallelogram).

4. 5 corners.

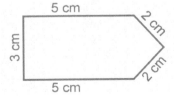

Shapes and Measuring Test, p. 33

1. a. rectangle b. triangle

2.

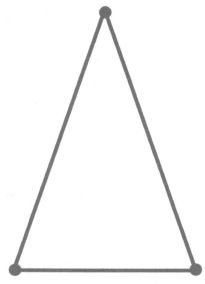

3.
The bottom side is 2 inches, the other two are 3 inches. It is a triangle.

4. a. 4 inches.

   b. 12 centimeters.

Mixed Review 5, p. 34

1. a. 0   b. 3   c. 5   d. 2

2.   4 – 6   2 – 0   6 – 9   8 – 4

3. a. twenty-nine   b. ninety-one   c. fifteen   d. fifty-seven

4.

Now it is:	a. 1:00	b. 11:30	c. 9:00	d. 6:30	e. 4:00
a half-hour later, it is:	1:30	12:00	9:30	7:00	4:30

5. Check the student's work. Answers will vary.

6.

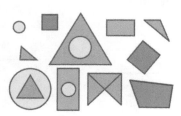

Mixed Review 5, cont.

7.

$9 - 5 = 4$	$3 + 4 = 7$	$10 - 2 = 8$
$3 + 1 = 4$	$8 - 1 = 7$	$3 + 5 = 8$
$10 - 6 = 4$	$0 + 7 = 7$	$9 - 1 = 8$
$2 + 2 = 4$	$9 - 2 = 7$	$2 + 6 = 8$

$9 - 3 = 6$	$3 + 2 = 5$	$10 - 7 = 3$
$3 + 3 = 6$	$10 - 5 = 5$	$3 + 0 = 3$
$10 - 4 = 6$	$0 + 5 = 5$	$7 - 4 = 3$
$2 + 4 = 6$	$9 - 4 = 5$	$2 + 1 = 3$

8. a. $30 < 38$ b. $87 > 85$ c. $69 < 96$ d. $58 > 56$

   e. $60 > 48$ f. $43 < 95$ g. $49 < 94$ h. $22 < 32$

Adding and Subtracting Within 0-100 Review, p. 36

1. YOU FOUND ALL OF THEM!

2.

a. $31 + 45$

$$\begin{array}{r} 3\ 1 \\ +\ 4\ 5 \\ \hline 7\ 6 \end{array}$$

b. $70 + 19$

$$\begin{array}{r} 7\ 0 \\ +\ 1\ 9 \\ \hline 8\ 9 \end{array}$$

c. $26 + 73$

$$\begin{array}{r} 2\ 6 \\ +\ 7\ 3 \\ \hline 9\ 9 \end{array}$$

d. $31 + 8$

$$\begin{array}{r} 3\ 1 \\ +\ \ \ 8 \\ \hline 3\ 9 \end{array}$$

e. $77 - 22$

$$\begin{array}{r} 7\ 7 \\ -\ 2\ 2 \\ \hline 5\ 5 \end{array}$$

f. $56 - 14$

$$\begin{array}{r} 5\ 6 \\ -\ 1\ 4 \\ \hline 4\ 2 \end{array}$$

g. $99 - 45$

$$\begin{array}{r} 9\ 9 \\ -\ 4\ 5 \\ \hline 5\ 4 \end{array}$$

h. $47 - 5$

$$\begin{array}{r} 4\ 7 \\ -\ \ \ 5 \\ \hline 4\ 2 \end{array}$$

3. b. You can use the method of finding the double and adding one for the problems below.

$5 + 5 = 10$
$6 + 6 = 12$
$7 + 7 = 14$
$8 + 8 = 16$
$9 + 9 = 18$

$7 + 8 = 15$ $6 + 7 = 13$

$6 + 5 = 11$ $8 + 9 = 17$

4. a. $9 + 9 = 18$ Doubles chart
   b. $8 + 4 = 12$ Trick with eight
   c. $9 + 5 = 14$ Trick with nine
   d. $7 + 7 = 14$ Doubles chart
   e. $7 + 8 = 15$ Just one more than a double
   f. $6 + 5 = 11$ Just one more than a double
   g. $3 + 9 = 12$ Trick with nine
   h. $6 + 7 = 13$ Just one more than a double

5.

a. $11 - 2 = 9$ $11 - 4 = 7$ $11 - 5 = 6$ $11 - 6 = 5$	b. $12 - 4 = 8$ $12 - 5 = 7$ $12 - 3 = 9$ $12 - 6 = 6$	c. $13 - 5 = 8$ $13 - 6 = 7$ $13 - 4 = 9$ $13 - 7 = 6$
d. $14 - 5 = 9$ $14 - 8 = 6$ $14 - 7 = 7$ $14 - 6 = 8$	e. $15 - 6 = 9$ $15 - 9 = 6$ $15 - 7 = 8$ $15 - 8 = 7$	f. $16 - 8 = 8$ $16 - 9 = 7$ $16 - 7 = 9$ $16 - 6 = 10$

6. a. Mariana read 15 books.
   b. Jose read 30 books.
   c. Janet read 10 more books than Jim.
   d. Jose read 10 more books than Janet.
   e. Answers will vary.

7. a. $20 - 2 - 5 = 13$ birds are left.   b. $5 + 1 + 3 = 9$ books.
   c. $20 - 14 = 6$ pages left.   d. $12 - 4 = 8$ Sam is eight years older.
   e. $\$11 + \$5 = \$16$. Yes, I will have enough with a dollar left over.

8.

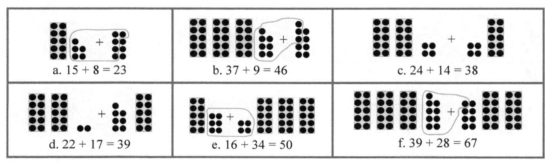

a. $15 + 8 = 23$ b. $37 + 9 = 46$ c. $24 + 14 = 38$
d. $22 + 17 = 39$ e. $16 + 34 = 50$ f. $39 + 28 = 67$

9.

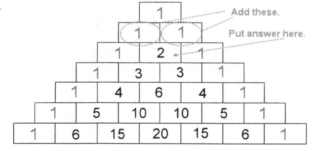

Add these.
Put answer here.

Puzzle corner

a.			b.			c.			d.			e.	

a.
4	5
− 2	3
2	2

b.
7	9
− 6	4
1	5

c.
3	6
−	4
3	2

d.
5	7
− 1	7
4	0

e.
6	7
− 1	5
5	2

Adding and Subtracting Within 0-100 Test, p. 40

1. a. 26, 46   b. 70, 86   c. 70, 10

2.

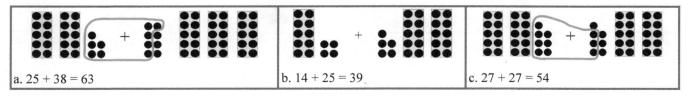

a. 25 + 38 = 63   b. 14 + 25 = 39   c. 27 + 27 = 54

3. a. 18   b. 13   c. 13   d. 15

4. a. 20 + 57   b. 78 − 44   c. 45 + 13   d. 87 − 20

	2	0
+	5	7
	7	7

	7	8
−	4	4
	3	4

	4	5
+	1	3
	5	8

	8	7
−	2	0
	6	7

5. Jake has more money (he has now $16). Jake has 4 dollars more than Jim.

Mixed Review 6, p. 41

1. a. 9:30   b. 12:30   c. 6:00   d. 3:30

2.

Now it is:	a. 2:00	b. 8:00	c. 12:00	d. 7:30	e. 10:30
half-hour later	2:30	8:30	12:30	8:00	11:00

3.

a.	b.	c.
100 − 1 = 99	10 − 1 = 9	10 + 90 = 100
90 − 2 = 88	20 − 2 = 18	20 + 80 = 100
80 − 3 = 77	30 − 3 = 27	30 + 70 = 100
70 − 4 = 66	40 − 4 = 36	40 + 60 = 100
60 − 5 = 55	50 − 5 = 45	50 + 50 = 100
50 − 6 = 44	60 − 6 = 54	60 + 40 = 100
40 − 7 = 33	70 − 7 = 63	70 + 30 = 100
30 − 8 = 22	80 − 8 = 72	80 + 20 = 100

4.

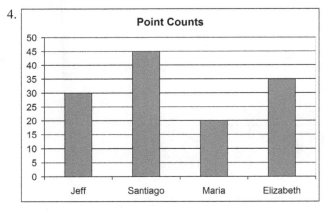

4. a. Jeff got ten more points than Maria.
   b. Santiago got ten more points than Elizabeth.

5. Answers will vary. Check the student's answers.

6. Answers will vary. Check the student's answers.

Mixed Review 6, cont.

7.

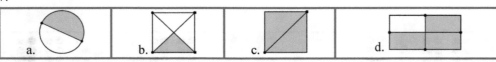

Puzzle corner:

+2	+3	+4
8 _10_	9 12	7 11
18 20	19 22	17 21
38 40	59 62	47 51
68 70	69 72	77 81
98 100	89 92	97 101

Mixed Review 7, p. 44

1.

a. 2 + 2 = 4 5 + 4 = 9	b. 2 + 5 = 7 0 + 5 = 5	c. 6 – 0 = 6 8 – 4 = 4	d. 3 – 1 = 2 10 – 3 = 7

2. a. 33   b. 86

3. 16, 26, 36, 46, 56, 66, 76, 86

4. a. $77 for both   b. $99 for both

5.

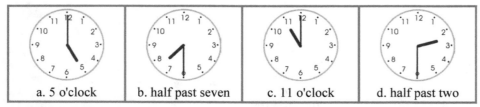

a. 5 o'clock	b. half past seven	c. 11 o'clock	d. half past two

6. a. A square or a rhombus.
   b. A triangle.

7.

a. 9 + 8 = 17 8 + 8 = 16	b. 9 + 3 = 12 8 + 4 = 12	c. 9 + 5 = 14 7 + 8 = 15

8.

a. 25 + 10 = 35 60 + 20 = 80	b. 90 – 30 = 60 100 – 70 = 30	c. 92 – 10 = 82 64 – 10 = 54

9.

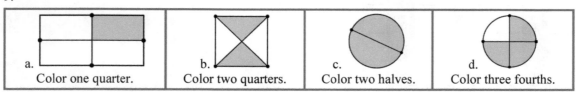

a. Color one quarter.	b. Color two quarters.	c. Color two halves.	d. Color three fourths.

10. They are equal.

11. a. cylinder   b. cube   c. cylinder   d. box

Coins Review, p. 46

1. a. 11¢   b. 27¢   c. 60¢   d. 32¢   e. 46¢   f. 87¢

2. a. two quarters, two pennies   b. two dimes, one nickel, two pennies <u>or</u> one quarter and two pennies
   c. three quarters, one penny   d. three quarters, one dime
   e. three quarters, four pennies   f. three dimes, four pennies

3. a. 56¢   b. 51¢

Coins Test, p. 47

1. a. 11¢   b. 34¢   c. 39¢   d. 42¢   e. 58¢   f. 102¢

2. Answers may vary. For example:
   a. Two quarters, one dime, and three pennies.   b. Three dimes, one nickel, and three pennies.
   c. Two quarters, one dime, one nickel, and four pennies.

3. a. 6¢ left.   b. 23¢ left.

Mixed Review 8, p. 48

1.

a.	b.	c.	d.
$10 - 1 = 9$	$8 + 9 = 17$	$25 - 10 = 15$	$52 + 7 = 59$
$8 - 2 = 6$	$7 + 8 = 15$	$38 - 10 = 28$	$35 + 3 = 38$
$7 - 3 = 4$	$5 + 6 = 11$	$100 - 10 = 90$	$26 + 2 = 28$

2.

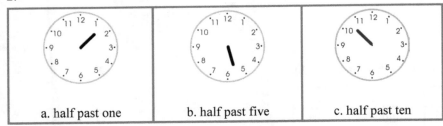

a. half past one	b. half past five	c. half past ten

3. Check the student's work.

4.

a. $15 - 7$	b. $14 - 9$	c. $16 - 8$
$15 - \underline{5} - \underline{2}$	$14 - \underline{4} - \underline{5}$	$16 - \underline{6} - \underline{2}$
$= \underline{8}$	$= \underline{5}$	$= \underline{8}$

5. a. 55   b. 85   c. 63   d. 42

6.

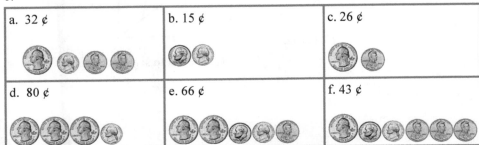

a. 32 ¢	b. 15 ¢	c. 26 ¢
d. 80 ¢	e. 66 ¢	f. 43 ¢

8. a. 26 ¢   b. 27 ¢

73

1. a. 5, 8, 7, 9   b. 10, 9, 9, 8   c. 8, 10, 7, 8   d. 10, 6, 10, 8

2. a. 5, 2, 4, 1   b. 2, 3, 3, 3   c. 4, 5, 1, 3   d. 7, 1, 2, 2

3. a. $2 + 7 = 9$; $7 + 2 = 9$; $9 - 2 = 7$; $9 - 7 = 2$

4. a. 5, 5   b. 7, 8   c. 2, 6   d. 5, 4

5. a. 27, 65   b. 50, 9   c. 0, 90

6. a. $16 < 26 < 61$ b. $14 < 51 < 54$

7. a. <   b. <   c. =

8. a. 88, 45   b. 76, 18   c. 79, 59

9. a. 50, 14   b. 52, 60   c. 26, 48

10. a. 49   b. 25   c. 96   d. 36

11. The child can circle some of the dots to make a ten in (a) and (b). That makes it easier to see the total.
    a. 53   b. 50   c. 49

12. $14 - 8 = 6$ or $14 - 6 = 8$

13. 20 more

14. Mark's cars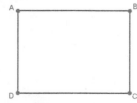
    Henry's cars

15. $10 - 6 = 4$ girls

16. The books cost $10 + $5 = $15. Andy has left: $20 - $15 = $5.

17. a. 8 spaces   b. 24 cars   c. 6 spaces

18. a. Isabelle has now 60 marbles.
    b. Her sister has 65 marbles.
    c. Her sister has more; five more marbles.

19. a. 11 o'clock, 11:00   b. half past one, 1:30   c. half past 8, 8:30

20.

Now it is:	a. 5:30	b. 7:00	c. 11:30	d. 12:00
a half-hour later, it is:	6:00	7:30	12:00	12:30
an hour later, it is:	6:30	8:00	12:30	1:00

21. a. ————————————————

    b. ————————————————

22. a.

(image not to scale)

22. d. triangles: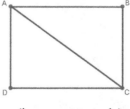

(image not to scale)

    b. a rectangle
    c. Side AB: _8_ cm   Side BC: _6_ cm

23. a. 18¢   b. 42¢   c. 85¢

24. 69¢

CPSIA information can be obtained
at www.ICGtesting.com
Printed in the USA
BVHW092300011019
559784BV00016BA/576/P